# OTHER BOOKS BY MARGE PIERCY

**Fiction**

GOING DOWN FAST
DANCE THE EAGLE TO SLEEP
SMALL CHANGES
WOMAN ON THE EDGE OF TIME
THE HIGH COST OF LIVING
VIDA

**Poetry**

BREAKING CAMP
HARD LOVING
4-TELLING *(with R. Hershon, E. Jarrett, and D. Lourie)*
TO BE OF USE
THE TWELVE-SPOKED WHEEL FLASHING
THE MOON IS ALWAYS FEMALE

**Play**

THE LAST WHITE CLASS *(with Ira Wood)*

# LIVING IN THE OPEN

# LIVING IN THE OPEN

## by Marge Piercy

ALFRED A. KNOPF    New York    1982

THIS IS A BORZOI BOOK
PUBLISHED BY ALFRED A. KNOPF, INC.

Copyright © 1969, 1971, 1972, 1973, 1974, 1975, 1976 by Marge Piercy

All rights reserved under International and Pan-American
Copyright Conventions. Published in the United States by
Alfred A. Knopf, Inc., New York, and simultaneously in Canada
by Random House of Canada Limited, Toronto. Distributed by
Random House, Inc., New York.

Grateful acknowledgment is made to the following magazines in which some of the
poems in this collection first appeared:

*Anon, Aphra, Atlantic Monthly, Bad Breath, Best Friends, Big Moon, Bosarts,
Boston Phoenix, Chomo-Uri, Clown War, Connections, Feminist Art Journal,
4-Telling, Good Times, Hampden-Sydney Poetry Review, Hanging Loose, Hearse,
Hellcoal Annual, Ironwood, Lamp in the Spine, Mosaic, New, New Salt Creek
Reader, Off Our Backs, Painted Bride Quarterly, Periodical Lunch, Ploughshares,
Poetry Now, Red War Sticks, Reflections, Rough Times, Seneca Review, The Second
Wave, Sojourner, Some, Street Cries, 13th Moon, Unmuzzled Ox.*

Library of Congress Cataloging in Publication Data
Piercy, Marge.   Living in the open.

   I. Title.
PS3566.I4L5        811'.5'4        75-37525
ISBN  0-394-73171-9

Manufactured in the United States of America

Published June 26, 1976
Reprinted Four Times
Sixth Printing, February 1982

For that patch of sand in which
I am unwisely but tenaciously rooted
like the salt spray rose;
for the people I live with
who help me to live;
for the women who help me know
how and why.

# CONTENTS

# HOMESICK

Finally I have a house
where I return.
House half into the hillside,
wood that will weather to the wind's gray,
house built on sand
drawing water like a tree from its roots
where my roots too are set
and I return.

Where the men rode crosscountry on their dirt bikes in October
the hog cranberry will not grow back.
This land is vulnerable like my own flesh.
In New York the land seems cast out by a rolling mill
except where ancient gneiss pokes through.
Plains and mountains dwarf the human, seeming permanent,
but Indians were chasing mammoth with Folsom points
before glacial debris piled up Cape Cod where I return.

The colonists found beech and oak trees high as steeples
and chopped them down.
When Thoreau hiked from Sandwich outward
he crossed a desert
for they had farmed the land until it blew away
and slaughtered the whales and seals extinct.

Here you must make the frail dirt where your food grows.
Fertility is created of human castings and the sea's.
In the intertidal beach around each sand grain
swims a minute world dense with life.
Each oil slick wipes out galaxies.
Here we all lie on the palm of the poisoned sea our mother
where life began and is now ending
and we return.

# FLAT ON MY BACK

The minutes are carried on the backs of elephants.
The glacial hours advance over the bed.
A day and a night:
a checkerboard of black and white nerves.

The sheets hatch crumbs and subtle wrinkles.
Reading too much makes my brain shrink from the skull.
Pain is a tunnel I have been going through.
Pain is a narrowing funnel.
Pain is a forcing sieve that turns me to gruel.

This time is in-valid.
I want to walk out.
I want to dance on the corpse of my fallen body.

Time was a fire scorching my back
that now is this icy muck enclosing me.
I want to burn again from the heels.
How beautiful is trouble
actively pursued.

# THE CLEAREST JOY

The clearest joy
is the ceasing of great pain.
When the iron bell rises from the head,
when the clanging shock subsides along the nerves,
when the body slides free
like a worm from a hook,
how the putrid city air
bubbles in the lungs.
Light glides in honey over the eyes.
The austere ceiling is made of meringue.
The body uncoils, uncoils
wonderfully empty like a lily.
Breathing is dancing.
Dumbly and wholly
like the basil plant on the sill
I lift my nose into the sun.

# MAKE ME FEEL IT

My head is full of folded linen.
My nerves are the bones of smelt.
If the hearts of the enemies of womankind
were served on plates with sauce vinaigrette
I would eat them and belch.
If the amber bodies of lively sensual boys
came leaping through my bed in dolphin schools
I would fuck them and yawn.
I am an unbaited mousetrap.
The fungus of boredom coats my tongue.
Friends step over me like a crack.
My head is a waitingroom in Dayton Ohio
where people in galoshes drowse under a stalled clock.

I need an old friend to drop dead so I may weep.
I need a good fighter to be murdered by the CIA so I may care.
The old sores are covered with scar tissue.
Once in Iowa City, Iowa in a friend's room
I found in his desk notes for an elegy
to be written on the death of Pound, his favorite poet.

A good thunderstorm of anger would galvanize me.
Ah, for a touch of the power coming through.
My lady, I am your hammer : make me ring against stone.
Mama, pick me up again and wear me,
I am your weapon.
My poetry and my politics have come unstuck.
Goddess, I am down to the brief hassles of the body,

the nerves struck like kitchen matches on the dark,
my wit which wants to diddle itself in the stacks of libraries.

Sweet mama, a life is as far as I can walk on it.
I have been lazy and lax,
I have been wanton and wobbly,
but take me up. Strop me.
Frighten the too easy wits out
till I leap and chatter and flash green,
let your hairy lightning blast me open and quaking.
I fear nothing like this silence
filled with the satisfied nibbling of myriad teeth
of the little appetites.

# I AWOKE WITH THE ROOM COLD

I awoke with the room cold and my cat
Arofa kneading my belly.
I had been walking around the lower east side
while from every alley and fruit market and stoop,
out from under the ravaged cars,
the cats came running to me.
All the cats had heard I was moving to the country
because of my lungs
and they began to cough and sneeze and whine.
All the starving rat-gnawed rickety spavined cats
of the lower east side with their fleas and worms
and their siren of hunger
followed me through the teeming blocks.
They threw themselves under the wheels of trucks
in an effort to keep up.
They were rubbing my ankles and yowling
that I must take every one of them along.
They wanted to breathe air that was not stained.
They wanted to roll on wet grass.
They wanted to chase a bird that wasn't a dirty pigeon.
Then the demands of the cats were drowned out.
As I ran, all of the eleven and twelve and thirteen year olds
who had died of skag in the smoking summer
began to miaou and miaou and miaou
till all of New York was white with pain like snow.

# GRACIOUS GOODNESS

On the beach where we had been idly
telling the shell coins
cat's paw, cross-barred Venus, china cockle,
we both saw at once
the sea bird fall to the sand
and flap grotesquely.
He had taken a great barbed hook
out through the cheek and fixed
in the big wing.
He was pinned to himself to die,
a royal tern with a black crest blown back
as if he flew in his own private wind.
He felt good in my hands, not fragile
but muscular and glossy and strong,
the beak that could have split my hand
opening only to cry
as we yanked on the barbs.
We borrowed a clippers, cut and drew out the hook.
Then the royal tern took off, wavering,
lurched twice,
then acrobat returned to his element, dipped,
zoomed, and sailed out to dive for a fish.
Virtue: what a sunrise in the belly.
Why is there nothing
I have ever done with anybody
that seems to me so obviously right?

## RIPTIDE

Ocean, mother of all living,
at the turning of the next tide, turn on us!
Reverse the rivers.
Loosen the silt in the stifled estuaries.
Up the grand canyon of the lordly stinking Hudson let it flow,
rolling up the Mississippi, thundering up the Columbia,
a tidal wave in the St. Lawrence, through the oily Cuyahoga,
all the poisoned fish, the cans, the plastic doilies,
iron ships of the black plague sunk in your belly,
innertubes and strontium 90 and rusting cars,
the chemical pissing of the miles of squatting factories.
Shoot it right back upstream,
into the tributaries, back through the dams, over the falls,
into the sewage systems and the pipes,
right up through the drains of every sink.

# COD SUMMER

June is the floodtide of green,
wet and lush and leafy, heavyladen.
In full summer the grass bleaches
to sand, hue of grasshoppers on the dunes.
The marsh begins to bronze.

Hot salty afternoons : the sun
stuns. Drops on our heads like a stone.
Among the pitch pines the sparse shade
simmers with resin,
crickets shiver the air.
The path is white sand shimmering
leading down from the hill of scrub oak
crusty with lichens, reindeer moss,
ripe earth stars scattering their spores.

Nothing commands the eye
except the sea at the horizon.
We must actively look : textures
of ground cover, poverty grass, bearberry,
lowbush blueberry, wood lily, Virginia rose.
The dusty beach plums range on the gnarled branch
from soft dull green through blush and purple
like a tourist's sunset in miniature.

Sandy, dwarfed, particular
this landscape yields nothing from a car.
A salt marsh must be learned on foot, wading,
lumbering in the muck, hopping tussocks of salt meadow grass,
hay arising sideways from last year's fallen harvest.
The marsh clicks and rustles
with fiddler crabs scuttling to their holes.
The blue-eyed grass has bloomed.
Now we find fat joints of samphire
turning orange, the intricate sea lavender.
Under us the tide undulates
percolating through the layers, slithering
with its smell of life feeding and renewing
like my own flesh after sex.

We go in this landscape together learning it
barefoot with our studious guides in a knapsack
catching Fowler's toads and letting them go.

# SAGE AND RUE

This afternoon I have been cutting herbs for vinegar:
the spicy warmth of basil lifting raggedy spikes,
the pinedark ferns and yellow umbrels of dill,
the rampant dense mints,
the coarse grassy leaves of tarragon
ruffled with dead stubs at the base.
In that harsh acid, the savor will be trapped and held.

I have been cutting herbs to dry in the shed,
making potpourri and tea for the winter,
picking over withered leaves from the racks.
The tedium of plucking into bottles soothes me.
My fingers smell of thyme and lemon verbena.

Though the flowers of chives are starry pink purple,
most herbs are weeds, flowers small and habit sprawling.
Bees hang on them, drunk with odors.
Other insects pass by, except jade-striped caterpillars
on the dill and the fennel who menace me with short
sticky horns erupting matter that would dissuade me
if I meant to eat them.

Herbs give sparingly. They will not sustain
you but render palatable what does.
They will heal, they will soothe, they will play
on your chemistry ringing small changes,
pleasure you in the bath and scent your clothes.

Asking little and slowly giving what no one needs
they thrive in poor soil under the blast of the sun.
Servants of witches, they draw cats.
Under the lovage my Persian washes a paw,
my Siamese is lounging debauched in the nepenthe, while an orange
stranger stalks a toad through the parsley and lilies.

I brush the rosemary with my scissors and sieve.
The small things of this world are sufficient and magical.
I praise the green power of fresh herbs
and the fragrant ghosts of dried, the redolent vinegars.
I praise things that remain themselves
though cut off from what fed them, through transformations.

# KNEELING HERE, I FEEL GOOD

Sand: crystalline children
of dead mountains.
Little quartz worlds
rubbed by the wind.

Compost: rich as memory,
sediment of our pleasures,
orange rinds and roses and beef bones,
coffee and cork and dead lettuce,
trimmings of hair and lawn.

I marry you, I marry you.
In your mingling under my grubby nails
I touch the seeds of what will be.
Revolution and germination
are mysteries of birth
without which
many
are born to starve.

I am kneeling and planting.
I am making fertile.
I am putting
some of myself
back in the soil.
Soon enough
sweet black mother of our food
you will have the rest.

# SEEDLINGS IN THE MAIL

Like mail order brides
they are lacking in glamor.
Drooping and frail and wispy,
they are orphaned waifs of some green catastrophe
from which only they have been blown to safety
swaddled in a few wraiths of sphagnum moss.
Windbreaks, orchards, forests of the mind
they huddle in the dirt
smaller than our cats.
The catalog said they would grow
to stand one hundred feet tall.
I could plant them in the bathroom.
I could grow them in window pots,
twelve trees to an egg carton.
I could dig four into the pockets of my jeans.
I could wear some in my hair
or my armpits.
Ah, for people like us, followed
by forwarding addresses and dossiers and limping causes
it takes a crazy despairing faith
full of teeth as a jack o'lantern
to plant pine and fir and beech
for somebody else's grandchildren,
if there are any.

# THE DAILY LIFE OF THE WORKER BEE

We breed plants, order seeds from the
opulent pornography of the catalogs,
plant, weed, fertilize, water.
But the flowers do not shine for *us*.

Forty days of life, working like a housewife
with six kids in diapers, at it like an oil rig pumping.
With condescension we pass on: busy as a bee.

Yet for them the green will of the plants
has thrust out colors, odors, the shapely trumpets and cups.
As the sun strikes the petals, the flower uncurls,
the bees come glinting and singing.

Now she crawls into the crimson rooms of the rose
where perfume reddens the air to port wine.
Marigolds sturdy in the grass barking like golden chow dogs
cry their wares to her. Enter. Devour me!
In her faceted eyes each image reverberates.
Cumulus clouds of white phlox
pile up for her in the heat of the sunburnt day.
The Madonna lily offers her pale throat.
Down into the soft well of the summer lilies,
cerise, citron, umber, rufous orange,
anthers with their palate of pollen
tremble as she enters.

She rubs her quivering fur
into each blue bell of the borage.
In the chamber of the peony she is massaged with silk.


Forty days she is drunk with nectar.
Each blossom utters fragrance to entice her,
offers up its soft flanks, its maddening colors,
its sweet and pungent fluids.
She never mates : her life is orgasm of all senses.
She dies one morning exhausted in the lap of the rose.
Like love letters turned up in an attic trunk
her honey remains to sweeten us.

# HEALING OF WEARINESS

On jagged weeks, my tongue blistered,
my nerves humming with a stench of burnt oil,
I am caught in too many separate battles.
Every message opens a new front in my skull.
I dream then of a feather cloudbed,
nestling in lavender downy quilt of oblivion.
My lids sink softly as big wet flakes of snow.

I want to be eaten by a TV set.
Sucked into a 3-D novel about the fourth planet of Deneb
with haploid and diploid generations.
I want to swim in the exotic stew of a stranger's trouble.
I want to make love with someone who speaks only skin.

I stalk into the marsh of the Herring River
and wait for the red-tailed hawk to show herself
riding the wind in broad arcs over the pitch pine.
The sky is low and spongy.
Fog breathes on my forehead.
I crouch watching brackish water inch up
the undercut banks on mud that smells like matches.
At the top of every scrub oak a red-winged blackbird
sits cocked like a ceramic piebird
while juicy song bubbles out.

I sit and I sit. My fingers web.
My back is wet and green in splotches.
My throat is cold and brimming as the river.

When I get up my calves ache.
I belong to battle as the heron to the reeds
till I give my body back.
I am shaped by my life, both twisted and straight.
Like the common blackbird I sit in the wind
scrapping for my food, my place, my kind
sometimes shrieking and sometimes singing.

# SAND ROADS

### 1. Sand roads

Each individually offers up
privy knowledge of a terrain.
I start with the whine of Route 6 in my ears.
In a while the pitch pines close around me,
small woods few bother to know
with their feet.

### 2. Woodcock alley

The curious mocking of the woodcocks
pursues us from the bushes,
a benign paranoia.
On an old house site the barberries
weave a barricade of intricate thorns.
The orange daylilies have been spreading
their ribbons of foliage, thrusting
their brief rough flowers to the bees
till they cover an acre: how to
measure the years
in the fibrous advance of the lilies.

### 3. River road, High Toss

In the reeds the blue
heron stalks, titled great
for his height, his antiquity,
that cool old lift of the heart
when he flies over the water

on ragged sails of wing
his big feet tucked but dragging.

The black ducks are maneuvering
in flotillas. On the narrow
rim at low tide are carved
the neat paw prints
of the raccoon where she washed her food.
The yellow-breasted chat
chucks from the briar.
Past the bridge where the
Herring River narrows
the sweetest and the
thorniest blackberries grow
in languid arches studded with spikes
trussed with long berries dripping juice
like a parable of pleasure and pain.


### 4. Paradise Hollow

Follow the old ruts,
circle the freshly fallen pine
broken in the last high wind,
stopping to free the young
sapling to rise again.
Follow the big friendly hands
like children's drawings,
of the sassafras. Filé gumbo.
Follow the ax cut path
narrower than your hips

through the labyrinth
of trees toppled years ago
in fire, the midden heap
of a farmhouse, daylilies,
broken plates of blue willow,
shells and rusted plow :
now the sumac tangles
wild and lacy over bones.

At the core of the hollow
the brook trickles
through a red maple swamp.
In winter we can hop
from mossy gray hummock to hummock
when the briar dies back.

Follow the brook to its source,
a spring in a meadow
still grassy from the
invisible house. The old apple
trees tall now as the black locusts
offer their gnarled and wormy
fruit like memories.

### 5.  The Old King's Highway

The Old King's Highway advances
almost in a straight line
up and down hill through

the white oaks and blueberry.
The banks are cut deep, erosion
softened by the curly
pubic beard of the mosses.

Rusted strands of barbed wire
hang from weathered posts
buried to their heads
in scrub oak.

Across the ruts marked
with tree roots like steps
the speckled toads hop.
Every while is a weathered
milestone like a miniature
grave marker. A bluejay
sits on one, blue
and loud as noon shouting its warning
THIEF        THIEF


### 6. Lombardy Hollow

Climb the hill past the beach
plums, frothy white or blossom
tinged with fuzz pink:
under the locusts where the grass
grows green and lush,
past the circular cellarhole
where they used to store potatoes,

cabbage, oysters awhile
stands a forest
of old lilacs.

Walk the road in May;
the poison ivy is still squat,
red and lets you pass.
Walk with your head tilted
back and let your wise nose
draw you to that odor.
Pass from house to house
like a peddler, like
a beggar. Not a board
remains unscavenged.
Yet you will find
the old hearths.
Lush as crinoline finery
lavender lace with its
strong green hearts of leaf,
its fragrance fiery sweet and sad
at its core, like a homemade
cordial for holidays,
coarse wood, longer lived
than the women who planted it
with work-pitted hands
by their kitchen doors.

## 7. The development

The bulldozers come, they rip
a hole in the sand along
the new blacktop road with a tony name
(Trotting Park, Pamet Hills)
and up goes another glass-walled-
split-level-livingroom-vast-as-a-
rollar-rink-$70,000-
summer home for a psychiatrist
and family.

Nine months vacation homes
stand empty except for mice
and spiders, an occasional
bird with a broken back twitching
on the deck under a gape of glass.

I live in such a development
way at the end of a winding
road where the marsh begins
to close in : two houses,
the one next door a local
fisherman lost to the bank
last winter, ours a box
half buried in the sand.
This land is rendered

too expensive
to live on. We feed
four people off it,
a kind of organic tall corn
ornery joke at road's end.
We planted for the birds cover
and berries, we compost, we set out
trees and at night
the raccoons come shambling.
Yet the foxes left us,
shrinking into the marsh.
I found their new den.
I don't show it
to anyone.
Forgive us, gray fox, our stealing
your home, our loving
this land carved into lots
over a shrinking watertable
where the long sea wind that blows
the sand whispers to developers
money, money, money.


## 8.  The road behind the last dune

Mostly you don't see the ocean
although when the surf is up
its roaring fills you
like a shell,

whistling through your
ears, your bones.
Nothing stands up here
but you, in the steady
rasp of the salt wind.
The oaks grow a foot high
dry gnarled jungles
you can't wade through
where eyes watch.
The hog cranberry bronze
in the fall, shines
metallically revealing
every hump of the sculptured hills.
The dune grass ripples
like a pelt, and around every
clump is traced a circle,
fingers of the wind.
Fox grape on the high dunes,
poison ivy whose bright berries
the birds carry in their bodies
to scatter, the dune
colored grasshoppers,
the fox with fur of fine sand.

You are standing too tall for
this landscape. Lie down.
Let the grass blow
over you. Let the plover
pipe, the kestrel stand beating its wings
in the air, the wolf spider

come to the door of its burrow,
the mouse nibble on
your toe. Let the beach pea
entangle your legs in its vine
and ring you with purple blossoms.

Now get up slowly
and seek a way down off the dunes,
carefully : your heavy feet
assault the balance.
Come down on the bench
of the great beach arching
away into fog.
Lie down before the ocean.
It rises over you, it stands
hissing and spreading its
cobalt hood, rattling
its pebbles.
Cold it is and its rhythm
as it eats away the beach,
as it washes the dunes out to sea
to build new spits and islands,

enters your blood and slows
the beat of that newish contraption
your heart controlling the waves
of your inward salt sea.
Shut your mouth. Keep still.
Let your mind open
like a clam when the waters
slide back to feed it.
Flow out to the ancient cold
mothering embrace, cold
and weightless yourself
as a fish, over the buried
wrecks. Then with respect
let the breakers drive you
up and out into
the heavy air, your heart
pounding. The warm scratchy sand
like a receiving blanket
holds you up gasping with life.

# THE HOMELY WAR

# ROUGH TIMES

*for Nancy Henley*

We are trying to live
as if we were an experiment
conducted by the future,

blasting cell walls
that no protective seal or inhibition
has evolved to replace.

I am conducting a slow vivisection
on my own tissues, carried out
under the barking muzzle of guns.

Those who speak of good and simple
in the same sandwich of tongue and teeth
inhabit some other universe.

Good draws blood from my scalp and files my nerves.
Good runs the yard engine of the night over my bed.
Good pickles me in the brown vinegar of guilt.
Good robs the easy words as they rattle off my teeth,
leaving me naked as an egg.

Remember that pregnancy is beautiful only
at a distance from the distended belly.
A new idea rarely is born like Venus attended by graces.
More commonly it's modeled of baling wire and acne.
More commonly it wheezes and tips over.

Most mutants die: only
a minority refract the race
through the prisms of their genes.

Those slimy fish with air sacs were ugly
as they hauled up on the mud flats
heaving and gasping. How clumsy we are
in this new air we reach with such effort
and cannot yet breathe.

## 16 IN '53

*for Jerry*

Your elephant adolescence in sandlots Brooklyn:
it sloshes like a washtub with nostalgia.
Heroes stalked in your attic dragging chains of words.
In the coalbin you lifted weights
your belly pink as strawberry ice cream.
You counted body hairs like daisies
foretelling love/notlove/notlove.
Pillows of snow, girls melted leaving damp rings.
At night a toad big as a gas storage tank,
you brooded over Flatbush muttering warts.
You lay in bed becoming snotgreen Dedalus:
you would not wash
wanting your Jewish mother to threaten you with rosaries,
excommunication, the hierarchic ashes of creaky saints.
In bed you were secretly thin with scorn
while your parents doted and fed you stuffed cabbage,
while outside the frowzy neighbors
browsing on newspapers and growing mad
with the cold dim light of television flickering in their eyes
danced, danced in the streets
for the burning to death
of Julius and Ethel Rosenberg.

# FALLING SONG

Wet, wet, in wetness I define you
in beer and milk and semen.
You are a waterspout with shaggy head of a rivergod
and red wine runs out of your mouth
and blood from your nose.
You are a humidifier combatting colds and dry sinuses
by continually giving off steam
and effluvia and rivulets of piss warm tears.
You take on a cold stagnancy,
you withdraw beneath slime,
you seep away.
You gather and fall suddenly with heat and noise
knocking everything flat.
Like a shrunken jellyfish,
like a beached salmon,
I fall into your gentleness
and am replenished.

# THE BIG ONE

My dear, you are a giant burr
caught in the world's short hairs.
You are a backporch floppy chair with stuffing
leaking out of your belly and all buttons gone
and when I plunk down
a cloud of dust hides me
and I rise up smelling of old dog.
My dear, you are a leaky red hot-water bottle.
You are a telephone that does not answer
unless I bash its head against the wall.
You are a bright yellow rose
the size of a boxer's fist.
This poem could go on as you must,
on through the marshes of your ennui.
You must get on with planting pits
in the bottom half of milk cartons and old galoshes,
squeezing poems out of the toothpaste tube of your guts,
crystallizing the best thoughts of all
out of the absolute zero
of the lonely night ice of vision.

# IMAGES EMERGING

In the closed box of the darkroom—
tepid air stirred by an exhaust fan,
stained by a dull orange safelight—
I am printing a roll from our last time.

In the developer
from the refrigerator door of the paper
ghostly you emerge grinning.
Slowly as I rock the tray
you come at me, hands extended.

Have I stolen a slice of you?
fixed you here?
It is sensual, to stand brooding
in the bathwater pool of the darkroom
rocking the trays in small waves
till you magically coalesce.

But the union is false. I look
but you do not see me.
Paper under my fingertips,
scent of acetic acid.
You are rocked in a bed two hundred miles
from here and your dark is peopled
with other faces.

## THERE IS NO KNOWN WAY
## TO TICKLE A CLAM

You say, things are getting better between us.
You shout that over your shoulder
as you race down an Up escalator
and out through a subway tunnel.
A train head on would scare you less than I
as I circle waving handkerchiefs and daisies.
You draw up your knees and turn clam.
You think I want to steal your soggy pearls.
Snap: you snip off my finger.
Do you think you could be eaten
whole? in parts? for breakfast?
You cannot remember who I am: fragments
break off and float loose
like something rotting under water.
Slimecold suspicion pumping through
washes the slight webs of affection away like waste.
Your shell builds involution upon involution
and you are closing down outer chambers of your mind.
Total defense
implies a dream of total surrender
but my hands are not tools for opening shells
and it was never my intention
to consume you.

## ALL CLEAR

Loss is also clearance.
Emptiness is also receptivity.
No, I cannot pretend:
the cells of my body lack you
and keen their specific hunger.
Yet, a light slants over this bleak landscape
from the low yellow sun,
a burning kite caught in the branches.
There is a lightness in me, the absence
of the weight of your judgment
bearing on my nape,
the slow stain of your judgment
rusting the moment.
I go out with empty hands
and women touch me, lightly, while we talk.
The words, the problems, the sharp faces
jostle like winter birds at a feeding station
although the crumpled fields look deserted.
I stroll in the cold gelid morning.

When it becomes clear I am not replacing you
don't think it is primarily
because you cannot be replaced.
Consider that I am taking pleasure
in space, visited but unoccupied
for every man I have loved
was like an army.

# TWO HIGHER MAMMALS

Each anniversary we share still
the attempt to grow, a politics
much too large for us
in which we rattle
wizened seeds in a beautiful gourd.
Even our cats are fussy eaters.
If only we were furry green chimps,
giant roseate thinking amoebae,
blue humanoids with quivering antennae
peaceful in instinct
and good to the core like bananas.

But we are woman and man,
other and murderous brother,
predators in whose fried brains
sputter all the raddled static
and greedy gobble of our race.
Faces of bored losers
yawn in our bones.

Loving leaves stretch marks.
Thinking clearly still hurts.
To be good for anything
is furious struggle
wrestling like dinosaurs
not only with the enemy
but with our own tough
and armored tails, weights
we drag behind.

# THE BOX

You are with me but gone.
Your skin grows bark. It
does not want to be translucent
to my touch.

I am a problem; you will solve me.
I am a demand; you will cancel me.
I am a shortage; you will audit me.

If I am green you crave purple.
If I am warm you sweat.
If I am round you bounce off.
The tides of my dreams
ruffle your sleep.
My loud needs slice like
helicopters through your air.

Sometimes you confuse me
with air, with water, with pollen,
the medium you live in,
with the clock of the heart
that runs slowly down,
with time that files
every hill flat.

To try cannot mean going backward.
The past is stored in our bones.
Do you want to walk onward
toward that blank wall?
Now we walk at the wall very fast
holding hands and trying to act as if
we believe in an opening.
If we come through the stone
we come through
in an unknown place.

# LIVING IN THE OPEN

**1.**

People ask questions
but never too many.
They are listening for the button to push
to make it go away.
They wait for me to confess
nights hollowed out with jealousy.

Or people say, Isn't that interesting
and believe nothing.
I must be public
as a dish of hors d'oeuvres on a bar.
I must hunt the shrubbery of couches for prey.
Loving not packaged in couples
shivers cracks down the closed world, the nuclear
egg of childhood, radioactive stone
at the base of the brain.

Can you imagine not having to lie?
To try to tell what you feel and want
till sometimes you can even see
each other clear and strange
as a photograph of your hand.

**2.**

We are all hustling and dealing
as we broil on the iron grates of the city.
Our minds charred, we collide and veer off.

46

Hard and spiny, we taste of DDT.
We trade each other in.
Talk is a poker game,
bed is a marketplace,
love is a soggy trap.

Property breeds theft and possession,
betrayal, the vinegar of contempt.
This woman, does she measure up?
This man, can I do better?
Each love is a purchase that can be returned
if it doesn't fit.

Hard as building a wall of sand.
Hard as gathering blackberries naked
in the thorny sprawl of a bramble.
Hard as saying I've made a mistake
and you were right.
How hard to love.
How painful to be friends.

My life frays into refuse,
parts of broken appliances,
into tapes recorded over, photographs
of people I no longer talk to
even on the phone.

How loud too the clash of my needs
in my pockets as I run to you

keys and coins jangling.
My hungers yowl and scrap in the gutter.
I will wring you for a few drops of reassurance.
My fears are telling the beads of your spine.
To hear your voice over the subway roar
of my will requires discipline.

No more lovers, no more husbands,
no masters or mistresses, contracts, no affairs,
only friends.
No more trade-ins or betrayals,
only the slow accretion of community,
hand on hand.

Help me to be clear and useful.
Help me to help you.
You are not my insurance, not my vacation,
not my romance, not my job, not my garden.
You wear your own flags and colors and your own names.
I will never have you.
I am a friend who loves you.

# CARRIED OVER MICHIGAN

Borne through the thin sky dragging a contrail
I sit over you swept forward,
a rabbit in the belly of a hawk.

You're there under the dirty unraveling wool of clouds
stuck up straddling a pole between your hard thighs
hair worn off by friction for pay
wrestling cables that speak flame.
While you shimmy only feet
into the icy wind, like a sailor on a mast,
I ride fathoms distant
in the upside down ocean of air.

The shadow of broad wings clumsy with engines
crosses your hunched shoulders
and hair of reindeer moss.
I am going someplace else for pay
west among strangers
where a bed waits
empty of you.

# JANUARY THAW

Six days
narrow as razors
yet wide enough
as that single bed
we slept on, tangled.

Deep enough to free fall
twined, dancing
through that huge temporary
space, wind whistling
the land turning
like the hands of a clock
the sun far below us.

Though dead winter
the chickadees are calling
as they do in spring
fe—ver, fe—ver rising,
descending sweetly.

A January thaw, country
roads turned chocolate pudding
our boots with sucking sounds
clambering over the still-
intact oak leaves
pages of an old diary
an old year
thrown off.

The air is Chablis.
The stinking Huron
we called the Urine, rages
in its ordered dirty banks
like a mountain stream.
The sun teases my arms.
Your mouth makes me drunk.
My body opens to a purple crocus.
Your hands on my back descend
a perfect scale.

You there, me here.
I bleed a slow
electricity of pain.
Six lean days
flashing like razors
and gone.

# I EVOKE THE GRAY FOX

How can I ask pity, gorged
with joy like a pigeon too fat to fly?
A boa constrictor who swallowed a cow,
I mean to coil round our stolen week.
Yet truly today I feel lean with missing,
flat as an envelope white and waiting,
an empty bathtub in a junkyard.

Your eyes of no color
your eyes of spring peepers that transmute on the hand
mossgreen into bronze into ashes,
strangers that cling to a glass door with starry feet,
waifs that leap thirty times their height.
Your eyes of water and sand,
of the dark belly of the wave cresting over me
as I plummet.

Fast-moving as the gray fox that climbs trees after squirrels,
lithe, straight, delicate in line, feathery
and strong as white pine.
I want to be with you walking the ties.
I want to be with you bumping in a truck on Michigan back roads.
I want to be with you on a mattress behind a padlock
while outside packs of commune dogs and children howl
for their supper and a piece of the action.
I am thirsty for your hands
light as water on me.
Your shadow is caught in my lashes,
I cannot blink free of its web.
How dull is a landscape without the clever feet of the fox
and the bark of his outlaw's laugh.

# THE BUMPITY ROAD TO MUTUAL DEVOTION

Do you remember the first raw winter
of our women's group, both of us fierce as mother bears?
Every day came down like a pile driver in the morning
shaking the bed empty
stomping sleep like a run-over bag.
Our pain was new, a too sharp kitchen knife.
We bled on everything we touched.
I could hardly type for scars.
Rage sang like a coloratura doing trills
in my head as I ricocheted up male streets.
You came on like a sergeant of marines,
you were freshly ashamed of your beauty
believing if you frowned a lot no one
would notice your face.
The group defined us the strong ones
loved us, hated us, baited us, set us
one on the other. We met
almost clandestinely. You brought flowers.
We praised lesbian love intellectually, looking
hard in each other's black eyes, and each stayed
on her side of the kitchen exuding
a nervous whine like an avalanche of white mice.

What a rutted road through thick gassy clouds of nightmare,
political bedlam. Each has let
the other down and picked her up.
We will never be lovers; too scared
of losing each other. What tantalizes past flesh
—too mirrored, lush, dark haired and soft in the belly—

is the strange mind rasping, clanging, engaging.
What we fantasize—rising like a bird kite
on the hot afternoon air—is work together.
Projects, battles, schemes, manifestoes
are born from the brushing of wills
like small sparks from loose hair,
and will we let them fade, static electricity?

What shall we do before
they crush us? How far will we travel
to no country on earth?
What houses should we build? and which tear down?
what chapels, what bridges, what power stations
and stations of that burning green energy
beyond the destruction of power?
Trust me with your hand. For us to be friends
is a mating of eagle and ostrich, from both sides.

# ON CASTLE HILL

As we wandered through the hill of graves,
men lost at sea, women in childbirth,
slabs on which were thriftily listed
nine children like drowned puppies,
all the Susan-B-wife-of-Joshua-Stones,
a woman in a long calico gown strolled toward us
bells jangling at waist, at wrists,
lank brown hair streaming.
We spoke to her but she smiled only
and drifted on into the overgrown woods.
Suppose, you said, she is a ghost.
You repeated a tale from Castenada
about journeying toward one's childhood
never arriving but encountering
on the way many people, all dead,
journeying toward the land of heart's desire.

I would not walk a foot into my childhood,
I said, picking blackberries for you to taste,
large, moist and sweet as your eyes.
My land of desire is the marches
of the unborn. The dead
are powerless to grant us
wishes, their struggles
are the wave that carried us here.
Our wind blows on toward those hills
we will never see.

# THREE WEEKS
# IN THE STATE OF LONELINESS

Here I am sitting like a side of beef in the middle of Kansas.
We've never been here together.
Nobody knows who I'm meaning
when I say your name like a charm.
It doesn't work.

Lawrence is lush in the gusty spring
with forsythia and redbud and flowering crab
all gorged with flowers at once
while lilacs begin to dye the air sweet as grape juice.
The leaves thrust open drooping as I watch.
From the limestone ridge of campus
I squint over the broad dusty bed of the farmlands.

What can give me a taste of you, touch of you?
The hazel glint of your eyes in a student's face.
A laugh in the hall makes me miss a beat.
In a man I am briefly holding
I touch that sad muscled exaggeration of caring
that makes you plod, a camel with nine humps of gloom
that you have not yet quite
perfected the world and yourself.
Not to share my thoughts sheers them off, unraveling.
I have no connections here; only gusty collisions,
rootless seedlings forced into bloom, that collapse.

56

The long distance bill keeps eating the food money.
I try to take an interest, I offer my finger to be chewed.
I lecture classes on why monogamy is wrong
while missing you sews a seam across my forehead.
I am the Visiting Poet : a red unicorn,
a wind-up plush dodo, a wax museum of the Movement.
People want to push the buttons and see me glow.

My loneliness lights up at night, a bucking neon cow
dropping purple moos on the sky of Kansas like blimps.
On the prevailing westerlies they should go sailing along
to be sighted looming across Massachusetts Bay dragging long groans
just about the time I'll be packing the troubles
I could or couldn't cause and getting ready to send
myself back to the center of my center,
open as a road and warm as a tongue,
my bed, my soil, my friend.

# PHASES OF THE SUN

July, full fat July
sweet as honeydew melon
cool breeze skimming foam off the sea
sun licking my skin
still as a cocoon on a branch
I lie, shaping invisible changes
in my head veined blue
as a cheese with dreams.

I need to be alone
yet missing you, it's
a thorn of pure sugar
piercing me.

A rhythm of here and gone
parting and closing
sliding shut and letting go,
our mating isn't a house
not even a trailer.

It's a path lit
by candles, one
for each bed we share,
votive offerings to the
proud eight-armed red
earth gods we are together.

# UNCLENCH YOURSELF

Open, love, open.
I tell you we are able
I tell you we are able
now and then gently
with hands and feet
cold even as fish
to curl into a tangle
and grow a single hide,
slowly to unknit all other skin
and rest in flesh
and rest in flesh entire.
Come all the way in, love,
it is a river
with a strong current
but its brown waters
will not drown you.
Let go.
Do not hold out
your head.
The current knows the bottom
better than your feet.
You will find
that in this river
we can breathe
we can breathe
and under water see
small gardens and bright fish
too tender
too tender
for the air.

# THE HOMELY WAR

**1.**

Wrote two letters while rain
trickled in lean streaks down my window.
One crowed of friends hiking, steamers, hot pie,
fat with bobwhite, peas planted and rhubarb dug in.
There are facts offered in the hand like ripe raspberries,
common phrases gentle as the caress of trailing hair.

The other malingered in a recitativo of wrongs,
counterpoint of minor and major abuse
quavering on a few tones of *No*.
A defense after my execution, a sense
that catches on the lip like a chipped glass
of having been used : used like a coin in a slot
or a borrowed towel slung sopping on a chair.
Tanglement that broke raw, in physical threat.
Months later the lies still come back
letters battered and stained, from a false address.

Happiness is simple
a box of sunshine
body against body, closed circuit of response.
Only misery is so complicated.

When another year turns over
compost in the pile
last year's feast breeding knots of juicy worms,
I do not want to be indicting
new accusations to another exlover
who has thrown off the scarlet cloak of desire to reveal
the same skeletal coldness, the need to control

60

crouching like an adding machine in his eyes,
the same damp doggy hatred of women,
the eggshell ego and the sandpaper touch,
the boyish murderer spitting mommy on his bayonet.
I am tired of finding my enemy in my bed.


## 2.

For two years I broke from these cycles, simply.
I thought the death of sex would quiet the air to crystal.
I would see what there was between women and men
besides itch, dependency, habit.

I learned less than I expected.
Judgment sat on my shoulder like a pet crow.
My dreams were skim milk and albumin.
I lacked irrational joy, a lion
lying on my chest purring, the hawk's talons and cry,
the coarse glory of the daylily that every midsummer morning
raises a new trumpet, that withers with dusk.
My head was severed like a flower in a glass
that would never make seeds.
Like an oak my tap goes deep,
more of me is in the earth than spread into air.
I think best rooted grappling past words.

Better, I thought, for me in my rough being
to force makeshift connections,
patches, encounters, rows,
better to swim in trouble like a muddy river rising

than to become at last all thesis
correct, consistent but hollow
the finished ghost
of my own struggle.


    **3.**

Madeline, in your purity I find myself rebuked.
Madeline, in your clarity I find myself restored.
You are the stream that breaks out
of a living tree; like the peach
you open your blossoms
to the wind that bears frost
a knife in its teeth,
you bloom in a ravaged landscape
black spring
old deaths coming to light
bones and split bellies of hunger,
the remaindered pages of the fall.
You stand and open from bare wood
fertile alone like the peach tree.
Long delicate leaves, slim green moons,
ripple over the sweet fruit
rounding on its stones.

You strike on marble at the core, rock
metamorphosed in pain and pressure,
the texture of agonized flesh.
You are vulnerable as the first buds of the maple
the deer arch their necks to crop.

Delicacy and honesty, unicorn and amazon wrestle
in your high sugar maple forest,
the Vermont hillside you love,
hard wood that drips sweetness you mistrust,
the symmetrical sculpture of each leaf,
the dome of the summer tree
heavy and dense as syrup, as sleep.

You grow deep into your rock, down into the cold
crevices of the fear of first and last things.
The stone of your death you crack and enter
with your lightning brain, with your fingers that ache.
Pain is the familiar whispering in your ear.

I come with my raggedy loves dragging
into the sphere of your clear regard.
I praise our common fight.
I praise friendship embarked on suddenly as a bus that arrives.
I praise friendship maturing like a tall beech tree.
I praise the differences that define us.
I love what I cannot be
as well as what I am.


**4.**

Seeking from women nurturance, feedback, idea,
my politics, my collective, why then this
open frontier with men? Yet I tell you in the other
I meet the dream exotic as a dragonfly's eye,

the grenade of a phrase, the joke that would never
leap the gap of the poles of my mind,
the angers struck unexpected
a spade clanging on rock in sand.
Talking without words on the body's drum:
it is flat, it is woody, it is lean as a shark's belly,
spiny as a sea urchin, leathery, gross, tulip sleek,
fur of the hare or wool of the sheep,
the toadstool of sex raising its ruddy bald head.
I find you beautiful, I find you funny, I find
you not translatable to words of my blood.
In that meeting I seep
out to the limits where my ego fades
into flesh, into electricity of the muscles thrumming,
into light patterns imploding on the nerves,
into the wet caves where my strength is born again.

I never want to merge: only to overlap,
to grow sensitive in the moment so that we move
together as currents, so that carried
on that wave we sense skin upon skin
nerve into nerve with millions of tiny windows
open to each other's light as we shine
from the nebulous center like squid
and then let go.

**5.**

I lack a light touch.
I step on my own words,
a garden rake in the weeds.
I sweat and heave when I should slip away.
I am earnest into sermons when I should shrug.
I ram on.

The inhabitants of my life change,
tides in a subway car.
At every stop coming and going.
What is constant except a few travelers
in the same direction, and the will to continue
through the loud dark
in the hope of someday arriving?

**6.**

My old friend, how we sustain
each other, how we bear witness.
We are each other's light luggage of essentials.
We are each other's film archive and museum
packed in the crumbling arch of the skull.
Trust is the slowest strength, growing
microscopic ring on ring of living wood.
The greater gift is caring,
the laying on of hands in the dark,
of words in the light.
The lesser gift is remembering,

the compass in the bush that makes clear the way
come, the way to go.
We have shaped each other.

My new friend, every beginning smells
like a sunny morning in a pine grove after rain.
The senses stretch out the necks of giraffes
for the smallest leaf of data to understand.
We give with the doors wide open;
a gardener with too many tomatoes,
we count nothing, we fill bushels with joy.
When does the tallying start?
Slowly underground fears begin, invisible
as the mycelium of a toadstool
waiting only for a damp morning to sprout.
I ask you to give much, to give up more.
What comes easy to a man comes
out of women. Nothing will be easy here.
Good will starts out fat and sweet
as tub butter and turns slowly rancid.
It must be made again daily
if we want it fresh.

The waters of trust run as deep as the river of fear
through the dark caverns in the bone.
Work is my center, my trunk
yet we are rooted in loving connection
with a deep grasping and full green giving.

## 7.

I am sick, sick to desperation
of the old defeats, of the broken treaties,
episodes of the same colonial war of women and men.
I want the cavalry to take off those bemedaled blue uniforms
the color of Zeus and those shiny boots clanking with spurs.
I want the horses to win this time and eat grass together.

In this movie the Army always comes bugling over the hill,
burns some squaws and pens up the rest on a reservation,
paves over the sacred dancing ground for a Stop and Shop,
and a ten-lane turnpike to the snowmobile factory.
Then they ask the doctor why nothing is fun.
Their eyes are the color of television screens.
They come by pretending, they die with their minds turned off.

Do you think on the tenting ground of General Bluster
young renegades may begin to steal away?
Or will they always go back for their paychecks?
The Indians anyhow are making alliance, forgiving
different tongues, paint jobs, tribal etiquette.
I think it is time for the extras to burn down the movie.

Yes, I am sick of treaties with the enemy who brings to bed
his boots and his law, who is
still and after my enemy.
I have been trained to love him, and he to use me.
Yes, I am weary of war where I want exchange,
sick of harvesting disgust from the shoots of joy.
Fight with my tribe or die in your blue uniform

but don't think you can take it off in bed.
It dyes your words, your brain runs cobalt
and your tear ducts atrophy to pebbles.

I love easily : never mind that.
Love is the paper script of this loose army.
Let us sleep on honesty at night like a board.
Talk with your body, talk with your life.
Grow me good will
rough and thick as meadow grass
but tend it like an invalid house plant,
a tender African violet in the best window.

# THE PROVOCATION OF THE DREAM

# THE TOKEN WOMAN

The token woman gleams like a gold molar in a toothless mouth.

The token woman arrives like a milkbottle on the stoop
coming full and departing emptied.

The token woman carries a bouquet of hothouse celery
and a stenographer's pad: she will take
the minutes, perk the coffee, smile
like a plastic daisy and put out
the black cat of her sensuous anger
to howl on the fence all night.

A fertility god serves a season
then is ritually dismembered
yet the name, the function live on:
so she finds the shopping lists
of exiled women in her coat pockets.

The token woman stands in the Square of the Immaculate
Exception blessing pigeons from a blue pedestal.
The token woman falls like a melon seed
on the cement: why has she no star shaped yellow flowers?
The token woman is placed like a scarecrow
in the longhaired corn: her muscles are wooden.
Why does she ride into battle on a clothes horse?
The token woman is a sandbag plugging
the levee: shall the river
call her sister as the flood waters rage?

The token woman is a black Chicana fluent in Chinese
who has borne 1.2 babies

(not on the premises, no child care provided)
owns a Ph.D., will teach freshmen English
for a decade and bleach your laundry
with tears, silent as a china egg.
Your department orders her from a taxidermist's catalog
and she comes luxuriously stuffed with goosedown
able to double as sleeping
or punching bag.

Another woman can never join her,
help her, sister her, tickle her
but only replace her to become her
unless we make common cause,
unless she grows out, one finger of a hand,
the entering wedge, the runner
from the bed of rampant peppermint
as it invades the neat clipped turf
of the putting green.

## BEauTIfUL WEEPER

Come under the willow
tree in the fall,
its yellow cataract
of languor: hair
of lady shuddering.
In the spring
the wands will brighten
early as forsythia.
Willow, willow by the water
your roots creep
into pipes and drains
to clog them
with your secret vigor.
Willow, willow shivering,
you look ethereal to survive,
you droop for a living
while underground your vast
root system thrives.
I want to be as little like you
as they will let me
except for your energy
striving for water to live,
willow,
sister willow.

# CONTRIBUTION TO OUR MUSEUM

I cannot worship ancestors.
All the tall ruffled ghosts
kept servants who pressed those linen shirts,
who murmur still in the carved and fitted stone
the life that was stolen from them.

In each cut diamond is hardened the anguish
carbonized of choking miners.
Each ruby bleeds the buried cries
of women who bloated with hunger after they harvested.
Each opal secretes the milky grief
of babies bombed sedately by computer
or spitted on bayonets in the Indian wars.

The gentry dance at the Diamond Ball at the Plaza
charitably, on behalf of third world education.
In the gutter the dead leaves scuttle,
the hungry rustle on the wind blowing
up from Bolivia, which the oil men own.

Always in the tidy fiefdoms of history taught
Louis on the guillotine is weighed in chapters
while fifty thousand peasants who starved
are penned in a textual note.
My folks were serfs, miners, factory women.
Their bent shoulders never bore the brocades in those cases.
They did not embroider the gossip at Versailles.
They were not invited to hunt with the czarina.

How can I love Mount Vernon
with its green alleys and its river perspective
and its slave quarters?
When the ghosts of Susan B. Anthony and Mother Jones,
of Harriet Tubman and Tecumseh and August Spies
dance on our small smokes as we picnic on the lawn,
we will preserve the slave quarters tenderly
because there are no more ghettos, no wage-slaves
and no soft domestic slavery bounded by rape.

The past leads to us if we force it to.
Otherwise it contains us
in its asylum with no gates.
We make history or it
makes us.

# THE LEGACY

Bury that family grandeur
of mink in mothballs,
rotting marble. Stop
lugging through furnished rooms
ancestral portraits
in a deck of marked cards.
Toss out those wroughtiron crutches.
Success like an incubus
visits your bed.
Nothing you do
will ever be enough.
You cannot win a prize
grand enough to ransom
your mother's youth.
The incense of those years
one by one guttered out
faint light, faint heat
chokes me in your room,
smothers you as you sleep
dreaming in hand-me-downs,
while dead women's wishes
like withered confetti
snow through your head.

# THE CONSUMER

My eyes catch and stick
as I wade in bellysoft heat.
Tree of miniature chocolates filled with liqueur,
tree of earrings tinkling in the mink wind,
of Bach oratorios spinning light at 33 1/3,
tree of Thailand silks murmuring changes.
Pluck, eat and grow heavy.
From each hair a wine bottle dangles.
A toaster is strung through my nose.
An elevator is installed in my spine.
The mouth of the empire
eats onward though the apple of all.
Armies of brown men
are roasted into coffee beans,
are melted into chocolate,
are pounded into copper.
Their blood is refined into oil,
black river oozing rainbows
of affluence.
Their bodies shrink
to grains of rice.
I have lost my knees.
I am the soft mouth of the caterpillar.
People and landscapes are my food
and I grow fat and blind.

# PEOPLE OF THE SHELL

Over the pebbles, the small bones
the slow night pours.
Sallow leaves float at the ceiling.
Brook trout stand on fins
like ballet dancers' feet.
My eyes pulse with ripples.
Currents roll me
languid as weed.

Then up from the bottom muck
you glide, rowing fast
with your great flippers
eyes glaring, chips of topaz
in the leather snout.

Grandfather snapping turtle
with ridged armor, the stout
plates dark with slime,
your ancient massive teeth
can crush bone.

Savage, silent you rise
cruising for flesh.
Your quick tongue tastes
the water for me.

Old gouger, tank heavy,
I know you, you spawned
me and turned away.
I have seen your gaping jaws
break water in the eyes
of a man lying over me.
You are stone that bites.

# A SHORT DARK TURNING

The full moon on the winter solstice
darkness at midafternoon
and the sea rising,
the gray creep of water through ditches
into lowlands and pasture,
the tentacles of the sea penetrate
where I have never seen water over the land.
The river brims
slapping the boards of the bridge.

Rain has come down wet month by month.
Other years, we counted raindrops like pearls,
we watched clouds scoot over on their way to the sea.
This is the year of the mushroom,
potato head sprouting in the path,
shelves crusting the fencepost,
toadstool erect between wet leaves.
Marshes lick their edges. Basements fill.

Not human justice but that of the earth,
the circle of all intertwined,
persuades me as Nixon bombs the dikes,
seeds the clouds with silver iodide
and nudges the typhoon off course for Hanoi,
great balances tip.
The wettest year since measurement began here.
Now the sea runs high on sodden land.
This is the season of low energy and a stingy sun.
The sky rattles old newspapers.

On Vietnam at the winter solstice
more bombs rain
than ever fell on people.
The wind is wet tonight off the gulf stream
with large warm drops like blood.
I am lettering a poster about the war.
For a moment I can't remember what year this is, dying.
A new year will be born from the waning moon
to carry hope like a tallow candle
in the bloody rain.
The sea is still rising.

# TO THE PAY TOILET

You strop my anger, especially
when I find you in restaurant or bar
and pay for the same liquid, coming and going.
In bus depots and airports and turnpike plazas
some woman is dragging in with three kids hung off her
shrieking their simple urgency like gulls.
She's supposed to pay for each of them
and the privilege of not dirtying the corporate floor.
Sometimes a woman in a uniform's on duty
black or whatever the prevailing bottom is
getting thirty cents an hour to make sure
no woman sneaks her full bladder under a door.
Most blatantly you shout that waste of resources
for the greatest good of the smallest number
where twenty pay toilets line up glinty clean
and at the end of the row one free toilet
oozes from under its crooked door,
while a row of weary women carrying packages and babies
wait and wait and wait to do
what only the dead find unnecessary.

# CIRCLING

*for Jeriann Hilderley*

The circle is centered on silence :
the cave in the heart of the rose,
the core of the apple where ebony seeds form,
the eye of the mandala where vision whites out.
The circle with no circumference is the pole
of journey and return in epicycles.

Praise what is round and holds us, bears us,
centered on the nipple, the navel, the cunt,
spheres of the hip, the head, the belly.
We rise and we set in the hill of sleep.
On the swelling earth we come and go into food.
Praise what opens, blooming, and gives way to seed.

Rose window, emblem of wholeness and our sex,
we seek to be healed to ourselves entire.
Each petal is a scene, we are stages of each other's journey.
There a crone with driftwood torso raises high a baby.
Mother and daughter embrace, no longer enemies
with the first month's blood.

We seek not rest but transformation.
We are dancing through each other as doorways.
We are ripples crossing and fusing, journeying and returning
from the core of the apple, the eye of the mandala,
the cave in the heart of the rose,
the circle without boundaries centered on silence.

# A PROPOSAL FOR RECYCLING WASTES

Victim not of an accident
but of a life that was accidental
she sprawls on the nursing
home bed: has a photo
of herself at seventeen with long
brown hair, face paprikaed
with freckles, like a granddaughter
who may live
in San Diego. In Decatur
love picked her up
by the scruff and after
out of work wandering dumped
her in Back of the Yards Chicago.
A broken nose, the scar of love;
stretch marks and a tooth lost
each child, love like
tuberculosis, it happens.
And generation used
her like a rutted highway
the heavy trucks trundling
their burdens all day and all
night. Her body was a thing
stuffed, swollen, convulsed
empty, producing for the state
and Jesus three soldiers and one
sailor, two more breeding wombs
and a (defunct) prostitute.

The surviving corporal drives
hack, one mother waits tables;
the other typed, married into
the suburbs and is den
mother to cubscouts.
The husband, cocksman, luckless
horse and numbersplayer, security
guard and petty thief, died
at fifty-two of cancer
of the colon.
Now like an abandoned car
she has been towed here
to fall apart.
She wastes, drugged,
in a spreading pool
of urine.
Surely she could be used,
her eyes, her heart
still strangely sturdy,
her one good kidney
could be salvaged for the rich
who are too valuable at seventy-four
to throw away.

# LOOKING AT QUILTS

Who decided what is useful in its beauty
means less than what has no function besides beauty
(except its weight in money)?
Art without frames: it held parched corn,
it covered the table where soup misted savor,
it covered the bed where the body knit
to self and other and the
dark wool of dreams

The love of the ordinary blazes out: the backyard
miracle: Ohio Sunflower,
                            Snail's Track,
                                        Sweet Gum Leaf,
            Moon over the Mountain.

In the pattern Tulip and Peony the sense
of design masters the essence of what sprawled
in the afternoon: called conventionalized
to render out the intelligence, the graphic wit.

Some have a wistful faded posy yearning:
                                        Star of the Four Winds,
            Star of the West,
                            Queen Charlotte's Crown.
In a crabbed humor as far from pompous
as a rolling pin, you can trace wrinkles
from smiling under a scorching grasshopper sun:

Monkey Wrench,
                   The Drunkard's Path,
                                    Fool's Puzzle,
          Puss in the Corner,
                        Robbing Peter to Pay Paul,
and the deflating
                   Hearts and Gizzards.

Pieced quilts, patchwork from best gowns,
winter woolens, linens, blankets, worked jigsaw
of the memories of braided lives, precious
scraps: women were buried but their clothing wore on.

Out of death from childbirth at sixteen, hard
work at forty, out of love for the trumpet vine
and the melon, they issue to us:
                        Rocky Road to Kansas,
          Job's Troubles,
                   Crazy Ann,
                        The Double Irish Chain,
          The Tree of Life:
                        this quilt might be
the only perfect artifact a woman
would ever see, yet she did not doubt
what we had forgotten, that out of her
potatoes and colic, sawdust and blood
she could create; together, alone,
she seized her time and made new.

# RAPE POEM

There is no difference between being raped
and being pushed down a flight of cement steps
except that the wounds also bleed inside.

There is no difference between being raped
and being run over by a truck
except that afterward men ask if you enjoyed it.

There is no difference between being raped
and being bit on the ankle by a rattlesnake
except that people ask if your skirt was short
and why you were out alone anyhow.

There is no difference between being raped
and going head first through a windshield
except that afterward you are afraid
not of cars
but half the human race.

The rapist is your boyfriend's brother.
He sits beside you in the movies eating popcorn.
Rape fattens on the fantasies of the normal male
like a maggot in garbage.

Fear of rape is a cold wind blowing
all of the time on a woman's hunched back.
Never to stroll alone on a sand road through pine woods,
never to climb a trail across a bald
without that aluminum in the mouth
when I see a man climbing toward me.

Never to open the door to a knock
without that razor just grazing the throat.
The fear of the dark side of hedges,
the back seat of the car, the empty house
rattling keys like a snake's warning.
The fear of the smiling man
in whose pocket is a knife.
The fear of the serious man
in whose fist is locked hatred.

All it takes to cast a rapist to be able to see your body
as jackhammer, as blowtorch, as adding-machine-gun.
All it takes is hating that body
your own, your self, your muscle that softens to flab.

All it takes is to push what you hate,
what you fear onto the soft alien flesh.
To bucket out invincible as a tank
armored with treads without senses
to possess and punish in one act,
to rip up pleasure, to murder those who dare
live in the leafy flesh open to love.

# FOR INEZ GARCIA

A woman's honor has been the possession
of her keeper, like the speed
of a race horse or the bloodline
of a pedigreed bitch, that no other man spoil
his wife, nor his ox, nor his ass.
Men have groomed their honor, embellishing it
in golden embroideries of legend heavy as iron gates;
have elaborated strict rituals of honor
armored in hierarchies of pain,
the samurai carving in his bowels and belly
a slow deep cross with his own blade.
The knight's *noblesse oblige* assumes the ignoble
obliged to bow and scrape and whine
if it please your honor, thanking your honor, please,
mercy! as fear rises like mud in the throat.

But what of my honor: Where do I draw
that red line, the perimeter of my will?
Am I everyman's urinal?
What does it mean to say No?
What does it mean to say No to superior force?

The man's body is a weapon and the woman's
a target. We are trained to give way.
Don't shout, let him win at tennis, don't boast
about your grades, don't argue,
give in, keep quiet, make peace.
Speak to the rapist nicely, speak softly
and reasonably, assure him you have
his best interests at heart. Kiss the knife.
Perhaps he will not injure you too much.

Perhaps he will not kill you today.
Perhaps the injury will close to scar tissue.
Perhaps you will forget to be afraid
the rest of your life, perhaps you will forget
what it is like to be used as a public toilet,
torn open like the throat
of a slaughtered calf.
Perhaps it would be good to open him.

To say Yes one must be able
to say No : No to the other,
the invader, the violator,
no. How does one say No
to superior force? The city is bombed
flat and taken, the field is pillaged
and burnt, the house is gutted. The woman
lies in the dust with her mouth
and cunt bleeding.

She rises. She rises to seize
the weapon and say again No
in blood. The only No that holds
is written in letters of bone.
Power accepts no lesser currency.

You cannot smoke your honor, you cannot
show it to your caseworker, you cannot
pay it in the supermarket for a can of beans.
Like freedom it doesn't exist
unless you make it. A woman's honor
is rooted in being able to say yes,

to say no and make each stick fast,
that ghostly will that rises in us
from the prone corpse of our passivity
like a resurrection, naked and thin and strange,
spirit of the responsible will
walking and talking from the grave
of the body that ate the child
that swelled into the woman, that now gives birth
to her own new holy being that carries high
a sword, a torch, a rifle. There is no
holiness without terror, no will
without responsibility and consequence,
no entire person without boundaries,
without doors that open and close
and the will to guard what goes
out and what comes in.

Let Inez Garcia, Joan Little become
two faces in a crowd of women, an army
each defending her body, defending her sister,
defending the frail ghost of the new whole
conscious self struggling to stand upright
and walk, like a nine month child.

# THE FEAR

I wake with tooth marks in my chest.
All day I feel something is missing.
I am not whole.
I must make from this soft body some useful thing
before I am eaten like an olive
and the pit of my bones spat out.
The minutes have tiny mouths of termites,
the day has shark's teeth,
and the vast night opens
like the jaws of a whale.

# LIES

**1.**

Always I feel it
bloating like a tumor
a weight, a shape
brushing my thighs
as I wade into sleep.

The water is warm like my blood
flat as a kitchen table.
My face dances there
in sun circles.
The water is a caress.
Then a fin breaks the surface
coming fast.


**2.**

You say I hate lying
because I want to be a child
holding my mother's hand.
You say no one needs to know
more than she needs.
You say, what is truth then?
Does it come in a package?
You say confession
is false orgasm.
You say feeding people part
of yourself is an attempt to bribe
them into love, you
there in the mirror.

94

**3.**

What I retain of my year with him
are the lies time has
filtered out in its coarse sieve
nuggets of fool's gold.
Every few weeks washes out another
to drop in my palm
bright, hard, worthless
yielding nothing but its own
nature, a dead end.

Strange to be left with his lies,
overnight constructions, the façades
of skyscrapers thrown up in panic,
Potemkin villages of the mind
forbidding the intimacy
he saw as invasion.
His best energy went into defense.
It is a poor creature like a slug
who builds the cathedrals of conch shell.
I perceive there is an aesthetic
of safety.

**4.**

Fear turns me nimble.
Chilled by coercion I flash
words, I glint facts, an acrobat
one-handed on top of a pike
juggling plates, balls and footstools

while sword dancing
with my toes and teeth.
One gauge of weakness
is to be forced to lie to a judge,
parent, caseworker, cop or other
thug of power.


**5.**

I live in a crazy house
with the blinds drawn tight
and the doors wide open.

Honesty is a compulsion swinging a
heavy sword like loving
like poetry itself.
I give too much importance to words
and my words define me.
I am always becoming words
that walk off as strangers.
Words, words, you sit, vultures eying my body.
You wait for my fat heart.
Isn't it enough that I spew all this paper?
What do I owe you
that I must try to love with words?
Sand in a sieve.

Lies catch in the teeth and rot there.
The truth goes down like water,
little taste, but
the stuff we're made of.

# HEAVY AS IN BEING SQUASHED

Coming down from the vault of the sky into New York
lowered sinking belly first
into the dead sea of carbon monoxide,
waste yellowing the air:
I descend in winged submarine through the murk
of that ocean
in which all life perishes.

Looking at those ziggurats
where symbolically the poor are sacrificed,
the actual deaths occurring offstage by computer,
I am overawed, I admit it.
I feel stalled
on a train between subway stations
suffocating.

The vast incomprehensible
inertia of what is
masses over me, impacts me.
Towers row upon spiky row
reduplicated like the banks
of teeth
in a shark's gullet:
tier over tier
for no earthly use
except counting, transferring
money from those who need
to those who don't.

This air crackles with power.
Matter is dense here,

light bends.
Despair is inertia,
looking out through the insect eyes
of surveillance at myself
as trapped object.

I carry hope
like a canary into the mines.
When it dies, I must move on.
What I hope on is that a rifle
in the hands of a young girl
brings down a bomber.
Every computer has a swing point
called a glitch
that builds error into each circuit
where we are encoded.
The irrational heart in us
is sun and fireball,
and the mind works as
razor, as clock, as wings.

I don't hope for justice
till we grow it,
only that for every action
comes a reaction equal
and opposite, and in the
dialectics of rebirth
the past never again
breaks from the egg.
Our every beginning
is a new place to be
under the canary yellow sun
of lion's burning mane and amber eye,
energy slanting dimly
through the veil of waste
to the rickety children
and hungry trees.

# FOR A BRAZILIAN 'BANDIT'

You are
no stronger than me:
your back hurt.
I lay down to show you
my morning exercises,
prayers of my body to survive,
the slow stretching
that strengthens my weak back.
When you tried
you shook with effort.

You are
no larger than me:
when I embraced you on parting
my arms doubled on your back.
I could lift you to my knees.
We could trade clothes.

The rifle is your weapon,
the typewriter mine.
Your way is harder.
My way is fatter.

You are no stronger,
no taller.
As I read the newspapers
I will remember.
Every time it is necessary
to do something hard
I will remember:

Your back is weak
your hands are small
your breasts are low and apart
your ankles are delicate
like mine.
We are fighting the same battle
and you also love roses,
write poems.

# PHYLLIS WOUNDED

To fight history as it carries us,
to swim upstream across the currents—no!—
to move the river, to create new currents
with the force of our arms and backs,
to shape this torrent as it shapes us
flowing, churning, dragging us under
into the green moil where the breath is pummeled
from the lungs and the eyes burst backward,
among rocks, the teeth of the white water
grinning like hungry bears,
ah, Phyllis, you complain too much!

We all carry in the gold lockets
of the good birthday child sentimental
landscapes in pale mauve where we have
everything we desire carried in on trays
serene as jade buddhas,
respectable as Jane Austen,
secure as an obituary in the *Times*.

We were not made for a heaven of Sundays.
Most people are given hunger, the dim pain
of being used twisting through the bowels,
close walls and a low sky, troubles visited
from above like tornadoes that level the house,
pain early, pain late, and a death not chosen.

My friend, the amazons were hideous
with the white scars of knife wounds,
the welts of sword slashes, flesh that would
remind nobody of a ripe peach.
But age sucks us all dry.

Old campaigners waken to the resonant singing
of angels of pillars of fire and pillars of ash
that only trouble the sleep of women
who climb on a platform or crouch at a barricade.
Your smile is rich with risk
and subtle with enemies contested.
Your memories whistle and clang and moan
in the dark like buoys that summon
and give warning of danger
and the channel through.

I was not born a serf bound to a ryefield,
I was not born to bend over a pressing machine
in a loft while the sun rose and set, I was not born
to starve in the first year with big
belly and spindly legs, I was not born
to be gang raped by soldiers at fourteen,
I was not born to die in childbirth,
to be burned at the stake by the Church,

but of all these we are the daughters
born of luck round as an apple
and fat as a goose, to charge into battle
swinging our great grandmothers' bones.
Millions of dead women keen in our hair
for food and freedom, the electricity
drives me humming. What privilege
to be the heiresses of so much wanting!
How can we ever give up?

Our laughter has been honed by adversity
till it gleams like an ax
and we will not die by our own hand.

# THE PROVOCATION OF THE DREAM

In the suburbs of the ganglia,
in the tract houses of the split-level brain,
in the bulldozed bowling alleys where staked saplings
shiver like ostriches in a zoo,
on streets empty of people
that dead-end at the expressway where cars bullet by,
in egg carton bedrooms, the dream is secreted.

On the clambering vines of the fingers
hard green dreams shape around seeds.
Sour enough to scald the tongue,
bitter with tannin and acid,
hard as granite chips, will these grapes ripen to give wine?

In the red Tau of the womb
dreams clot, clump, a dense pale smear
like a nebula.
Who has known this woman?
This woman has known herself.

It is the wind impregnated me,
the wind galloping with tangled mane through the brush
breaking twigs, with burrs snarled in her coat.
The wind fills me, I am her sail and shoot before.
The wind comes through the tawny grass
parting it like a comb
and enters me.

Six hours after I had dropped acid
I began to labor. I was brought to a room with men
and a woman who belonged to the men.
Mosquito fears bothered them.
They held me down till my muscles tore
but I was granted blindness.
The drum of my uterus pounded.
The fist of my womb clenched and unclenched
on me, in the surging cave.
Death crooned under the roar of the waterfall
calling to the child to rest, to stay, to sleep;
calling to the mother to falter, to sink, to fade.

Weeping and screaming I gave birth, I was born.
When I came down
I was handed shame like a cup of sour coffee
for the noise I had made when I had not known them,
when I had been knowing myself.
In the proper ritual we change roles and give assistance.
We bring each other through on that wind.

In the dim tunnels of library stacks
the dream is laid in the spines of books
like the eggs of beetles, in fairy stories,
broken statues and painted vases, mythologies,
legends of queens, old wives' tales.
The eggs hatch larvae who chew and change.

The dream advances like a wave of purple dye
through the conduits of the blood.

The vision alters dreams till the night is hung
with bold faces painted on shields,
the voices of women like bright scarves on the wind,
the cries of women wet as blood,
women who dance in fire burning and charred
but still dance
together.

I wait for the dream to enter the brain
and turn on the power to connect,
clearing the roads of the instincts.
The fountains will run water and the fruit of the senses
offer its sweetness and knowledge on every stall.
The office workers will go out to the green belt to plant
and the peasants of the belly will also give law.

I wait for the dream to reach the eyes
and shatter the mirror where the moon of the face
eclipses energy's sun.
I wait for the dream to reach the belly
and make us serious as lean gray wolves
whose shadows race far behind as they hunt.
I wait for the dream to enter the muscles
till we ride our anger like elephants into battle.

We are sleepwalkers troubled by nightmare flashes.
In locked wards, we closet our vision, renouncing.
We turn love loud on the radio to shut out cries in the street.
Ours is the sleep of objects given, sold, taken, discarded,

a shuddering sleep whose half remembered dreams
are cast on the neat lawn of the domestic morning,
red blossoms torn by a high wind from a crab apple tree.
Only when we break the mirror and climb into our vision,
only when we are the wind together streaming and singing,
only in the dream we become with our bones for spears,
we are real at last
and wake.

## A Note About the Author

"I was born in Detroit, Michigan, and left when I was seventeen. I've lived mainly in Chicago, Brooklyn, Manhattan, San Francisco, and Boston, always in the center of cities until I moved to Wellfleet on Cape Cod in 1971. I have been a political activist for years—civil rights, anti-war groups, SDS from 1965–69. Since 1969 I have been active mainly in the women's movement, which has been a great energy source (as well as energy sink!) and healer of the psyche for me. I live off my writing and travel a lot giving readings and workshops."

## A Note on the Type

This book was set on the Linotype in Century Expanded designed in 1894 by Linn Boyd Benton (1844–1932). Benton cut Century Expanded in response to Theodore De Vinne's request for an attractive, easy-to-read typeface to fit the narrow columns of his *Century Magazine*. Early in the nineteen hundreds Morris Fuller Benton updated and improved Century in several versions for his father's American Type Founders Company. Century remains the only American type face cut before 1910 still widely in use today.

Composed, printed, and bound by The Haddon Craftsmen, Scranton, Pennsylvania. Typography and binding design by Virginia Tan. Photographs by Bob Frankel.